SRA Art Connections

Level 1

Authors

Rosalind Ragans, Ph.D., Senior Author

Willis Bing Davis
Tina Farrell
Jane Rhoades Hudak, Ph.D.
Gloria McCoy
Bunyan Morris
Nan Yoshida

Contributing Writer

Patricia Carter

Music Center Education Division
The Music Center of Los Angeles County

**SRA
McGraw-Hill**

Columbus, Ohio

A Division of The McGraw-Hill Companies

Credits

SRA/McGraw-Hill

*A Division of The **McGraw·Hill** Companies*

Copyright © 1998 by SRA/McGraw-Hill.

Send all inquiries to:
SRA/McGraw-Hill
250 Old Wilson Bridge Road
Suite 310
Worthington, Ohio 43085

Printed in the United States of America.

ISBN 0-02-688315-5

3 4 5 6 7 8 9 VHP 04 03 02 01 00 99 98

Authors

Senior Author
Dr. Rosalind Ragans, Ph.D.
Associate Professor Emerita
Georgia Southern University

Willis Bing Davis
Art Department Chair
Central State University, Ohio

Tina Farrell
Director of Visual and Performing Arts,
Clear Creek Independent School District, Texas

Jane Rhoades Hudak, Ph.D.
Professor of Art
Georgia Southern University

Gloria McCoy
K-12 Art Supervisor,
Spring Branch Independent School District, Texas

Bunyan Morris
Demonstration Art Teacher
Marvin Pittman Laboratory School,
Georgia Southern University

Nan Yoshida
Former Art Supervisor,
Los Angeles Unified School District, California

Contributors

 ARTSOURCE Music,
Dance, Theater Lessons
The Music Center of Los Angeles County
Education Division, Los Angeles, California
Executive Director, Music Center Education
Division-Joan Boyett
Concept Originator and Project Director-
Melinda Williams
Project Coordinator-Susan Cambigue-Tracey
Arts Discipline Writers:
Dance-Susan Cambigue-Tracey
Music-Rosemarie Cook-Glover
Theater-Barbara Leonard
Staff Assistance-Victoria Bernal
Logo Design-Maureen Erbe

More About Aesthetics
Richard W. Burrows, Executive Director, Institute for
Arts Education, San Diego, California

Safe Use of Art Materials
Mary Ann Boykin, Visiting Lecturer, Art Education;
Director, The Art School for Children and Young
Adults, University of Houston-Clear Lake,
Houston, Texas

Museum Education
Marilyn JS Goodman, Director of Education,
Solomon R. Guggenheim Museum,
New York, New York

The National Museum of Women in the Arts Collection
National Museum of Women in the Arts,
Washington, DC

Contributing Writer
Patricia Carter
Assistant Professor of Art Education
Georgia Southern University

Reviewers
Mary Ann Boykin
Visiting Lecturer, Art Education;
Director, The Art School for
Children and Young Adults
University of Houston-Clear Lake, Houston, TX

Judy Gong
Multi-age Classroom Teacher
Pacific Elementary School
Lincoln Unified School District
Stockton, CA

Lori Groendyke Knutti
Art Education
Harrison Street Elementary School
Big Walnut Elementary School
Sunbury, OH

Claudia Moody-Jones
Mentor Teacher
L.A. Unified School District
Los Angeles, CA

Steven R. Sinclair
Art Teacher
Big Country Elementary School
Southwest Independent School District
San Antonio, TX

Rebecca Wall
First/Second Grade Teacher
Good Elementary School
Carrollton-Farmers Branch I.S.D.
Carrollton, TX

Student Activity Testers
Grant Crawford
Heather Swaggerty
Lauren Haupt
Andrew McMillian
Jessica Strayer

TABLE OF CONTENTS

Unit 1 Line

Unit 2 Shape

Unit 3 Color

Unit 4 Space and Form

Unit 5 Texture and Rhythm

Unit 6 Emphasis, Balance, and Unity

More About . . .

What Is Art?

Art is...

Painting

Leonardo da Vinci. (Italian). *Mona Lisa.* c. 1503–1506. Oil on wood. $30\frac{1}{2} \times 21$ inches. Louvre, Paris, France. Erich Lessing, Art Resource, NY.

Drawing

Leonardo da Vinci. (Italian). *Self Portrait.* 1414. Red chalk. Royal Library, Turin, Italy. Scala, Art Resource. NY.

Architecture

Waddy Wood. (American). *National Museum of Women in the Arts.* Washington, DC. Photo by Dan Cunningham.

Sculpture

Helen Cordero. (American). *Storyteller Doll.* From the Girard Foundation Collection, Museum of International Folk Art, Santa Fe, New Mexico. Photographer: Michael Monteaux.

Printmaking

Katsushika Hokusai. (Japanese). *The Great Wave Off Kanagawa.* 1831–33. Polychrome woodblock print. $10\frac{1}{8} \times 14\frac{15}{16}$ inches. Metropolitan Museum of Art, New York, New York.

Weaving

Artist unknown. Ashanti people (Ghana). *Kente cloth.* From the Girard Foundation Collection, Museum of International Folk Art, Santa Fe, New Mexico. Photographer: Michael Monteaux.

Pottery

Lucy Leuppe McKelvey. (American). *Whirling Rainbow Goddesses.* (*Top view*). Clay. $6\frac{3}{4}$ inches high, 12-inch diameter. Keams Canyon Arts and Crafts. New Mexico.

Clothing

Artist unknown. (China). *Chinese Children's Slippers.* 1991. Cotton appliquéd with silk. $4 \times 2 \times 1\frac{1}{2}$ inches. Hudak private collection. Photography ©Tom Amedis.

Art is created by people.

Art talks with . . .

Line

Shape

ColoR

SPACE

FORM

TEXTURE

Rhythm

Balance

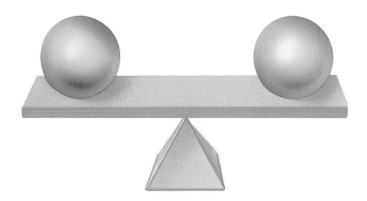

Emphasis

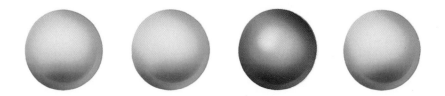

Unity

An Introduction to
Line

Albrecht Dürer. (German). *The Great Piece of Turf/Albertina Vienna.*
1503. Watercolor and tempera on paper, mounted on cardboard.
40.3 × 31.1 cm. Erich Lessing/Art Resources, NY.

Artists use many kinds of lines in their artwork.

What kinds of lines do you see in this painting?

Artist Profile

Albrecht Dürer
1471–1528

Self Portrait.

Albrecht Dürer

- was a German artist.
- was a printmaker.
- created art about many subjects.

Lines

Joaquin Torres-García. (Uruguayan). *New York City—Bird's-Eye View.*
c. 1920. Gouache and watercolor on board. $13\frac{1}{2} \times 19\frac{1}{2}$ inches. Yale University
Art Gallery, New Haven, Connecticut. Gift of Collection Societe Anonyme.
©1998 Artists Rights Society (ARS), New York/ADAGP, Paris.

This painting has different lines
in it. Can you find thick, thin, rough,
smooth, broken, and solid lines?

Seeing like an artist

Look around.
Can you find lines
like you saw in
the painting?

A line is a mark made by a tool as it moves.
Here are different ways that artists change lines.

thick   thin   smooth   rough   solid   broken

Create

How many different ways can you use a line?

Think of all the ways you have used lines.
Create a design with lines.

Ty Brannen. *Age 7. Line City.* Oil pastel and watercolor.

Calm Lines

Wolf Kahn. (American). Study for *Chesapeake and Ohio Canal in Spring II.* 1986. Oil on canvas. 30 × 52 inches. Courtesy of Wolf Kahn and D.C. Moore Gallery/© Licensed by VAGA, New York, NY.

What kind of lines did this artist use to make the land and water? What kind of lines make the trees?

Seeing like an artist

Look out a window. What has lines like the painting?

Artists use **vertical** and **horizontal** lines to make a picture look calm.

vertical   horizontal

Create

Where is your favorite quiet place outside?

Think of lines you see there.
Use calm lines to paint your place.

Anna Pofer. Age 7. *My Place*. Tempera.

Diagonal Lines

Vincent van Gogh. (Dutch). *Bedroom at Arles.* 1888. Oil on canvas. $29 \times 36\frac{5}{8}$ inches. Art Institute of Chicago, Chicago, Illinois. Helen Birch Bartlett Memorial Collection.

This artist uses many diagonal lines in his painting. Can you find them?

Seeing like an artist

Look around. Where do you see diagonal lines?

Lines that look like they are falling down or getting up are called **diagonal**. They give a busy feeling to artwork.

Create

What does your room look like?

Think of the lines you see in your room.
Paint your room using diagonal lines.

Ellen Manor. Age 6. *Bedroom. Tempera.*

Curved Lines

Agnes Tait. (American). *Skating in Central Park*. 1934. Oil on canvas. $33\frac{7}{8} \times 48\frac{1}{8}$ inches. National Museum of American Art, Smithsonian Institution, Washington, DC.

This painting has many curved lines. Trace one with your finger.

Seeing like an artist

Look around for curved lines. Where do you see them?

Artists use **curved lines** to show movement.

Create

What would a painting of you playing a game look like?

Think of the lines your movements make.
Draw yourself playing your favorite game.

Morgan Bowers. Age 7. *One Fall Day.* Oil pastel.

Buildings Have Lines

Lawren S. Harris. (Canadian). *Shacks.* 1919. Oil on canvas. 107.9 × 128 cm.
National Gallery of Canada, Ottawa, Ontario, Canada.

These houses have many kinds of lines. Which lines did the artist use for the windows, doors, and roofs?

Seeing like an artist

Look at pictures of buildings. Find the important lines.

Artists who draw and plan **buildings** are called **architects**. They use lines to draw buildings.

vertical   horizontal   diagonal

Create

What kinds of lines would you see in a playhouse or tree house?

Imagine you are designing one.
Create your own playhouse or tree house.

Julie McElwain. Age 7. *My Clubhouse.* Construction paper and marker.

Lines Show Movement

Jacob Lawrence. (American). *Children at Play.* 1947. Tempera on Masonite panel. 20 × 24 inches. Georgia Museum of Art, University of Georgia, Athens, Georgia. Eva Underhill Holbrook Memorial Collection of American Art. Gift of Alfred H. Holbrook.

Name the different line directions you see in the painting. Which lines help you know that the girls are moving?

Seeing like an artist

Play "Freeze!" Ask a partner to name the lines you make.

Artists use some lines to show movement in their artwork.

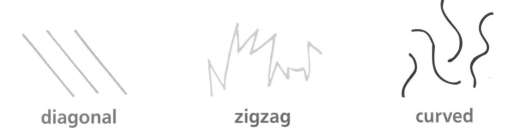

diagonal   zigzag   curved

Create

How many different ways can you move?

Think of the lines that show these movements.
Use these lines to draw yourself.

Laura Lopez-Blanquez. Age 6. *Dancing.* Watercolor.

Lines in Dance

Tandy Beal & Company: Dancers performing an excerpt from "Dust to Dust."

Tandy Beal has her dancers move. Then they "freeze." The lines of their bodies change. The dance shows that body lines create pictures.

What To Do

Use pasta shapes to design a dance.

1. Use your body to show how each pasta shape looks.

2. Pick three pasta shapes. Show how each shape moves.

3. Work with a group. Put all your pasta shapes and movements together to make a dance.

Extra Credit

Use your body. Show the difference between uncooked and cooked pasta.

Line

Reviewing Main Ideas

There are many kinds of lines.

Artists use lines to show movement
and to express feelings.

Antoine Watteau. (French). *Happy Age, Golden Age.* c. 1716–17. Oil on wood.
$8\frac{1}{4} \times 9\frac{5}{8}$ inches. Courtesy of the Kimbell Art Museum, Fort Worth, Texas.

Let's Visit a Museum

This museum is in Fort Worth, Texas. Many paintings and sculptures are exhibited there. The museum also has art workshops for children.

Summing Up

*T**his** artist used many lines to paint the picture.

How many kinds of lines can you find?

Kimbell Art Museum, Fort Worth, Texas.

Unit 2

An Introduction to
Shape

Artist unknown. Kuna (Panama). *Mola.* 1995. Layered and cut fabric
with stitchery. 42 × 66 inches. Georgia Southern University, Statesboro, Georgia.
Permanent Collection. Photograph © by Frank Fortune.

A shape may be either a **geometric shape** or a **free-form shape**.

geometric shape   free-form shape

Create

What different kinds of shapes would you put in a rug?

Think of your favorite shapes. Design a rug with many shapes.

Madison Hollingsworth. Age 6. *My Christmas Carpet,* Construction paper and marker.

People Shapes

Carmen Lomas Garza. (American). *Naranjas (Oranges)*. Gouache. 20 × 14 inches. Collection of Mr. and Mrs. Ira Schneider, Scottsdale, Arizona. Photo by Wolfgang Dietze.

The artist used free-form shapes to paint these people. Where are the people? What are they doing?

Seeing like an artist

Trace in the air the outline of your teacher. What kind of shape did you make?

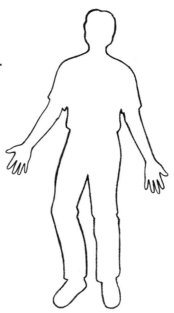

The human body is a **free-form shape**.

Create

What would your shape look like if a partner traced you?

Think of your body outline.
Paint a free-form picture of yourself.

Jesse Drewa. Age 7. *Jesse.* Watercolor.

Action Shapes

Jacob Lawrence. (American). *Builders—Red and Green Ball.* 1979. Gouache on paper. 30 × 22 inches. Courtesy of the artist and Francine Seders Gallery LTD., Seattle, Washington. Photo by Chris Eden.

What are the people doing in this painting? Find the people building something from wood. Is anyone standing still?

Seeing like an artist

Move one hand in the air. How does the shape of the hand change?

Changing the **position** of body parts can show how people move.

Create

How do you move when you work?

Think of the positions of your body parts. Paint a picture of yourself at work.

Olivia Hartsell. Age 6. *Ballet Dancer.* Crayon and watercolor.

Outlining Shapes

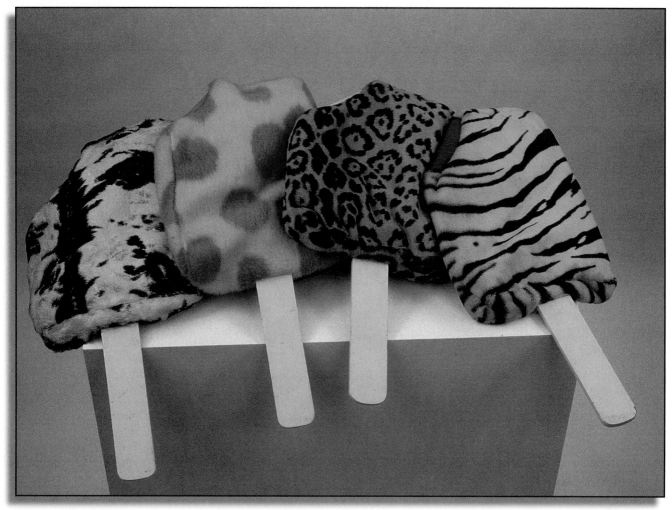

Claes Oldenburg. (Swedish). *Soft Fur Good Humors.* 1963.
Fake fur filled with kapok and wood painted with enamelin.
$2 \times 9\frac{1}{2} \times 19$ inches. Courtesy Claes Oldenburg.

Trace with your finger the outline
of an ice-cream bar shape in the picture.
Is it a geometric or a free-form shape?

Seeing like an artist

Trace the sole of
your shoe. What
kind of shape is
the outline?

The shape of an object is drawn with an **outline**

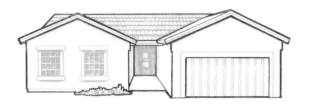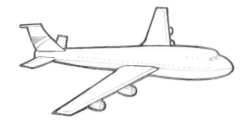

Create

How are the shapes of food different?

Think of some meals you like.
Draw the outline of your favorite food.

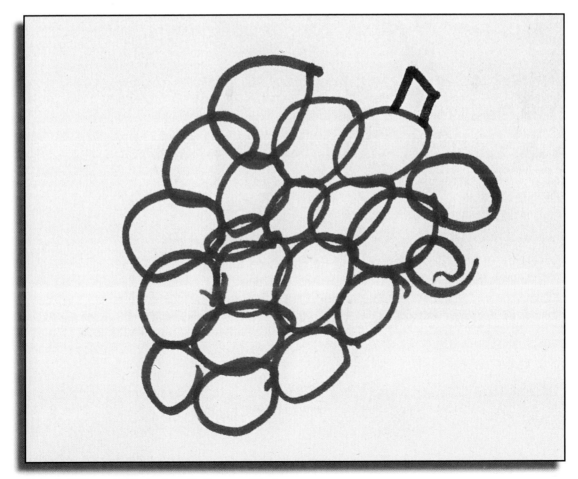

Crystal Hernandez. Age 7. *Grapes.* Marker.

Still-Life Shapes

A still life is a picture of things that do not move. What fruit shapes did this artist choose? What else do you see in the painting?

Roy Lichtenstein. (American). *Cubist Still Life*. 1974. Oil and magna on canvas. $90 \times 68\frac{1}{16}$ inches. National Gallery of Art, Washington, DC. Gift of Lila Acheson Wallace. © 1996 Board of Trustees, National Gallery of Art, Washington, DC.

Seeing like an artist

Look for a still life at home. Is there a bowl of fruit or a plant on a table?

A still life has **geometric** and **free-form shapes**.

Create

What kinds of objects would you place in a still life?

Think of all the different shapes you see.
Paint your own still life.

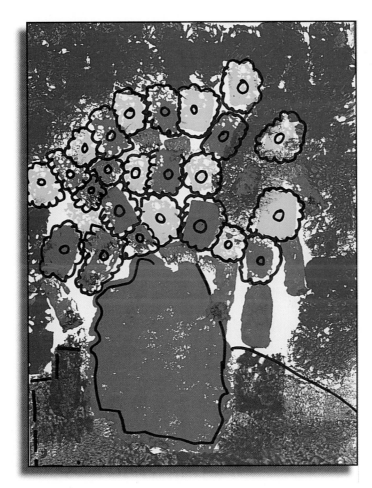

Kwamaine Rhodes.
Age 6. *Sunflowers in Red Vase.* Tempera and marker.

Moving Shapes

Henri Matisse. (French). *Circus, Plate II from Jazz.* 1947. Pochoir, printed in color. $16\frac{5}{8} \times 25\frac{5}{8}$ inches. Museum of Modern Art, New York, New York. The Louis E. Stern Collection. Photograph © 1998 The Museum of Modern Art, New York. © 1998 Succession H. Matisse, Paris/Artists Rights Society (ARS), New York.

This artist used bright colors and moving shapes in his painting. Point to the free-form shapes.

Seeing like an artist

Find magazine pictures showing free-form shapes in action.

Artists use **free-form shapes** to show the action of people moving.

Create

How does music make people move?

Think of how you move when dancing.
Make a cut-paper picture of people dancing.

Ellen Drott. Age 7. *Dancing for Joy*. Cut paper.

Shapes in Acting

Little Theatre of the Deaf: Ensemble using American Sign language.

Actors in "The Little Theatre of the Deaf" put on plays. They use body actions, words, and sign language. They also show how machine parts might look and move.

What To Do

Use your body to show parts of an object.

1. Think about a fire engine.

2. Tell what you might do and say to act like a fire engine.

3. Work with a group. Use your bodies and voices to show a fire engine.

Extra Credit •

Create another machine with your group. Perform it for the class.

Shape

Reviewing Main Ides

A shape may be geometric or free-form.

People are free-form shapes.

Charles Burchfield. (American). *Noontide in Late May.* Watercolor and gouache on paper. Collection of Whitney Museum of American Art, New York, New York/Purchase/Photography by Geoffrey Clements.

Careers in Art

Tamera and Michael Stocker are married. They work at Disney Studios in California. They are both animators. An animator draws the pictures for animated movies and TV shows.

Summing Up

***L**ook* at the shapes in the painting.

Where do you see geometric shapes? Where are the free-form shapes?

Tamera and Michael Stocker, animators

An Introduction to
Color

Mary Cassatt. (American). *Susan Comforting the Baby.* 1881. Oil on canvas. $25\frac{5}{8} \times 39\frac{3}{8}$ inches. Houston Museum of Fine Arts, Houston, Texas. The John A. and Audrey Jones Beck Collection.

Artists mix some colors to make other colors.

This artist uses many colors.
Name the colors you see in the artwork.

Artist **P**rofile

Mary Cassatt
1847–1926

Mary Cassatt

- was an American.
- painted mothers and their children.
- used paint and pastels.

A Rainbow of Colors

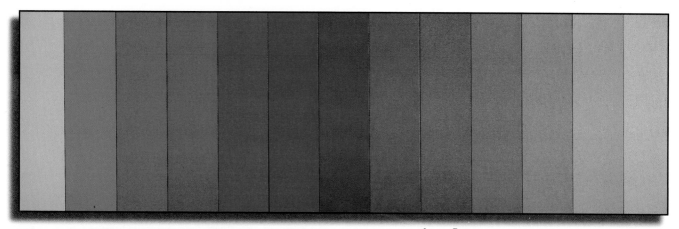

Ellsworth Kelly. (American). *Spectrum III*. 1967. Oil on canvas. $33\frac{1}{4} \times 9\frac{5}{8}$ inches. The Museum of Modern Art, New York, New York. The Sidney and Harriet Janis Collection. Photograph ©1998 The Museum of Modern Art, New York.

This artwork is about rainbow colors. Point to each color as you say its name.

Seeing like an artist

Find something in the room for each rainbow color.

A **color wheel** shows the colors of the **rainbow** in order.

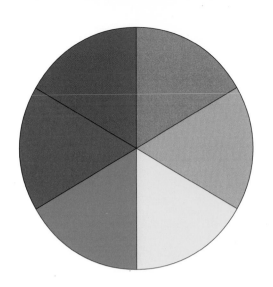

Create

How would you change the colors of things around you?

Think of something you would like to make colorful.
Draw a rainbow world.

Jessica Brubaker. Age 7. *Colors.* Crayon and Watercolor.

Primary Colors

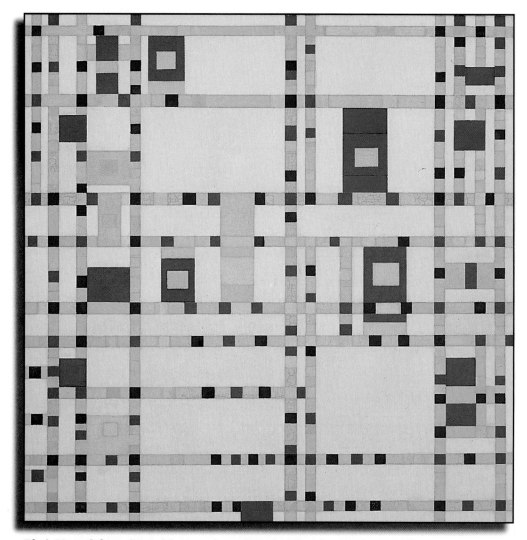

Piet Mondrian. (Dutch). *Broadway Boogie-Woogie*. 1942–43. Oil on canvas. 50 × 50 inches. The Museum of Modern Art, New York, New York. Given anonymously. Photograph © 1998 The Museum of Modern Art, New York.

This picture is made with only primary colors and white. What colors do you see?

Seeing like an artist

What primary colors are fire engines, police uniforms, and school buses?

Red, yellow, and blue are **primary colors**.

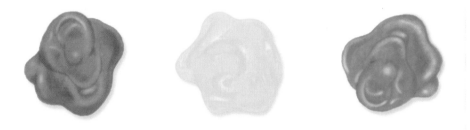

Create

Where would you use primary colors in a design of your own?

Think of a way to design your colors.
Cut paper into a primary color design.

Brianna Ruch. Age 6. *Shapes Dance*. Cut paper.

Red and Yellow Make Orange

Artist unknown. (Ecuador). *Man's Headband of Toucan Feathers.*
Courtesy of the Smithsonian National Museum of the American
Indian, New York, New York. Photo by David Heald.

This headband has red and
yellow feathers. Where do you
see orange feathers?

Seeing like an artist

How many different
orange objects can
you find in the
room? Name them.

Red and yellow are **primary colors**. They can be mixed to make the **secondary color** orange.

Create

How many shape colors can you make using only yellow and red?

Think of a shape for yellow and one for red.
Paint a shape picture.

Seth Afman. Age 6. *Shapes*. Tempera.

Blue and Yellow Make Green

Marc Chagall. (Russian). *Peasant Life*. Oil on canvas. $39\frac{3}{8} \times 31\frac{1}{2}$ inches. Albright Knox Art Gallery, Buffalo, New York. Room of Contemporary Art Fund, 1941/©1998 Artists Rights Society (ARS), New York/ADAGP, Paris.

This painting is made with rainbow colors. The green was made by mixing blue and yellow. What did the artist paint with each color?

Seeing like an artist

Collect some green leaves. Arrange them from lightest to darkest green.

Blue and yellow are **primary colors**. They can be mixed to make the **secondary color** green.

Create

What colors do you see most in a park?

Imagine a summer day outside.
Draw a green scene.

Dustin Durrence. Age 7. *Green Frog*. Oil pastel.

Red and Blue Make Violet

Hans Hofmann. (German). *Rhapsody.* 1965. Oil on canvas. $84\frac{1}{4} \times 60\frac{1}{2}$ inches. Metropolitan Museum of Art, New York, New York. Gift of Renate Hofmann, 1975.

This painting uses colors and shapes to tell about musical sounds. What colors and shapes do you see? What do you think violet, red, and blue sound like?

Seeing like an artist

Look around your classroom. What do you see that is violet?

Red and blue are **primary colors**. They can be mixed to create the **secondary color** violet.

Create

What would a violet creature look like if you saw one on the street?

Imagine its shape and size.
Design a very violet creature.

Matthew Fitzgerald. Age 7. *Violet Vern.* Tissue paper and wax paper.

Primary and Secondary Colors

This painting has primary and secondary colors. Name the two primary colors the artist mixed to make each secondary color.

Thomas Hart Benton. (American). *July Hay.* 1943. Oil and egg tempera on composition board. 38 × 26¾ inches. Metropolitan Museum of Art, New York, New York. George A. Heam Fund, © 1988 T. H. Benton and R. P. Benton Testamentary Trusts/ Licensed by VAGA, New York.

Seeing like an artist

Name things in your room with primary colors. Name things with secondary colors.

The three **primary colors** can be used to create three **secondary colors**.

Create

What kinds of things did you see on your way to school?

Think of all the shapes and colors.
Paint a landscape.

Oliver Sandoval. Age 6. *Passing Landscape.* Tempera.

Color in Music

"Cajun Medley." AMAN International Folk Ensemble, John Zeretzke.

The Cajuns live in Louisiana. They play music on fiddles and guitars. Long ago they began to use spoons and other to to add a lively beat to their music.

What To Do

Make musical instruments.

1. Play rhythms with pans, spoons, and other things. Play loudly and softly. Play quickly and slowly.

2. Play a rhythm pattern. Have a friend play it back. Take turns.

Extra Credit

Play along to a song you know.
Ask some friends to play with you.

Color

Reviewing Main Ideas

Red, blue, and yellow are
primary colors.

Artists mix primary colors to
create secondary colors.

Mark Rothko. *Orange and Yellow*. 1956. Oil on canvas,
91 × 71 inches. The Albright-Knox Art Gallery, Buffalo, New York.

Let's Visit a Museum

This museum is in Buffalo, New York. It has a large collection of modern art. The museum has exhibits of student art every year.

Summing Up

*T*his artwork is full of color.

Which two primary colors did the artist mix to make orange?

Albright-Knox Art Gallery, Buffalo, New York.

Unit 4

An Introduction to
Space and Form

Artist unknown. (Polynesia). *The Giant Stone Moai.* c. A.D. 1000–1500, restored 1978. Ahu Nau Nau, Easter Island, Polynesia. Volcanic stone (tufa), average height approximately 36 feet.
© George Halton/Photo Researchers, Inc.

A form has height, width, and depth.

Look at these two pictures.
They are 3-D forms.

What surrounds each stone form?

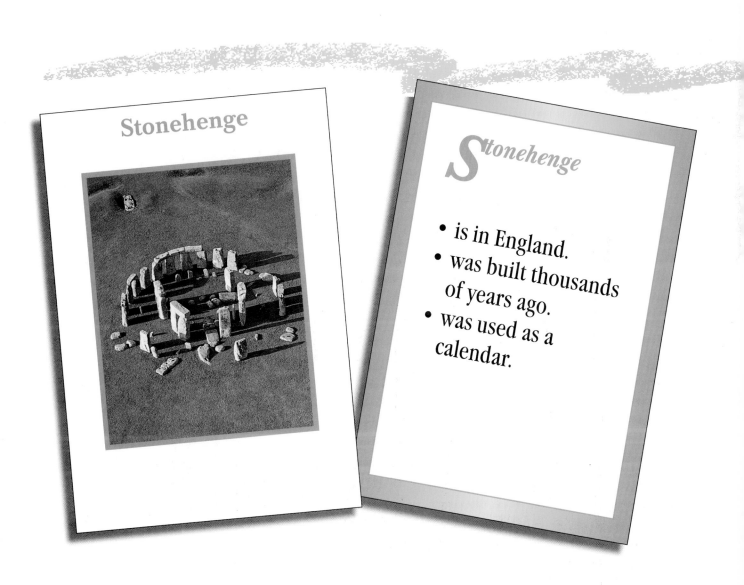

Stonehenge

Stonehenge

• is in England.
• was built thousands of years ago.
• was used as a calendar.

Shapes and Forms

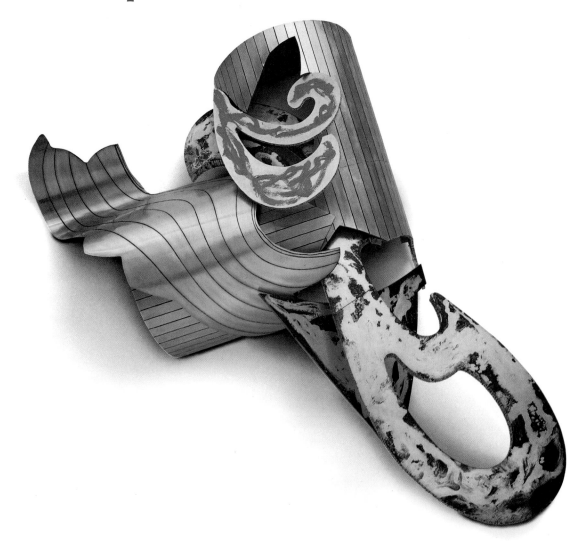

Frank Stella. (American). *Loomings 3X*. 1986. Ink and oil paint on etched magnesium and aluminum. $142\frac{1}{8} \times 162\frac{1}{2} \times 44$ inches. Walker Art Center, Minneapolis, Minnesota. Gift of Joan and Gary Caspen. 1987/©1998 Frank Stella/Artists Rights Society (ARS), New York.

Look at how all the different shapes and forms were combined in this artwork. Point to the empty spaces created by them.

Shapes have **height** and **width**.
Forms have height, width, and **depth**.

Create

How would you combine shapes and forms in your artwork?

Think of shapes you'd like to use. Design a mobile.

Jessica Strayer. Age 6. *Mobile*. Cut paper.

Forms Take Up Space

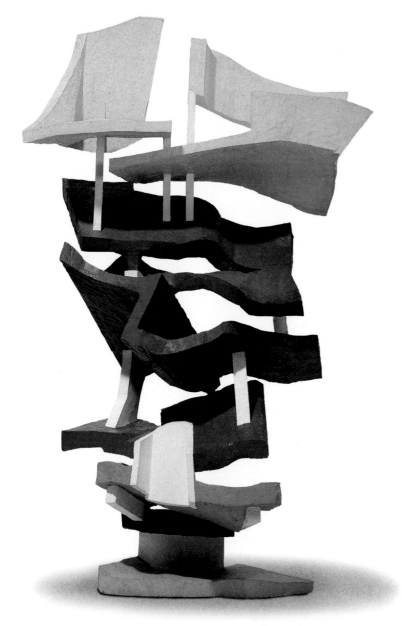

George Sugarman. (American). *Yellow Top.* 1959. Acrylic on laminated wood. 89×46×34 inches. Walker Art Center, Minneapolis, Minnesota. Gift of the T.B. Walker Foundation, 1966.

This sculpture has forms. It also has open spaces for air to go through. Point to the open spaces.

Seeing like an artist

You are a form in space. If you move, do you change the space?

A form takes up **space** and has space all around it. A form can also have space inside it.

Create

What can you design that takes up space?

Think of the forms you will use. Create a sculpture.

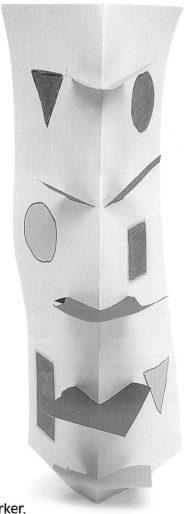

Carrie Lorenzo. Age 6. *Tall Thing*. Cut paper and marker.

Lesson 2

Free-Form Forms

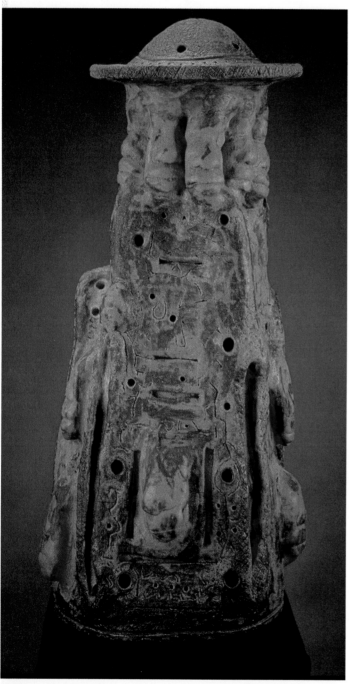

Trees and people are free-form forms. So is this sculpture. What would it look like from each side?

Nathaniel Bustion. (American). *Brownstone Series.* Earthenware, ash glaze. 37 × 20 × 16 inches. Private Collection.

Seeing like an artist

Sketch an outline of a free-form form you see every day.

Some forms are **geometric forms**.
Other forms are **free-forms**.

Create

What would a sculpture look like from all sides?

Think of the shapes you would see.
Design a free-form sculpture.

Emmanuel Ross. Age 7. *The May Flower.* Modeling compound.

3-D Me!

Helen Cordero. (American). *Storyteller Doll.* Museum of International Folk Art, Santa Fe, New Mexico. From the Girard Foundation Collection in the Museum of International Folk Art, a unit of the Museum of New Mexico. Photographer: Michael Monteaux.

Some statues honor famous people. This statue is a storyteller doll. Whom do you think the artist wants to honor?

Seeing like an artist

This statue has many small forms. What are they?

A person has **height**, **width**, and **depth**.
A person is a **3-D form**.

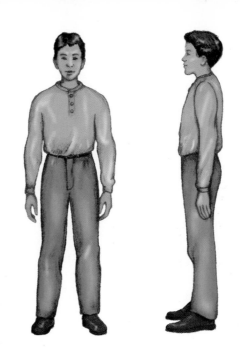

Create

What do you think you look like from different sides?

Think of your dimensions.
Create a statue of you.

Madeline Jobrack. Age 6. *Resting.* Clay.

Buildings and Spaces

Artist unknown. *Corn Palace.* c. 1892. Mitchell, South Dakota. ©Peter Pearson/Tony Stone Worldwide.

This building is made up of many different forms and open spaces. Find five different forms and two open spaces.

Seeing like an artist

Have you ever seen a building with forms like the building pictured?

Buildings are made from **3-D forms**. The forms have open spaces for people to move through.

Create

What would the home of an imaginary creature look like?

Think of the different forms and spaces. Design a home for an imaginary creature.

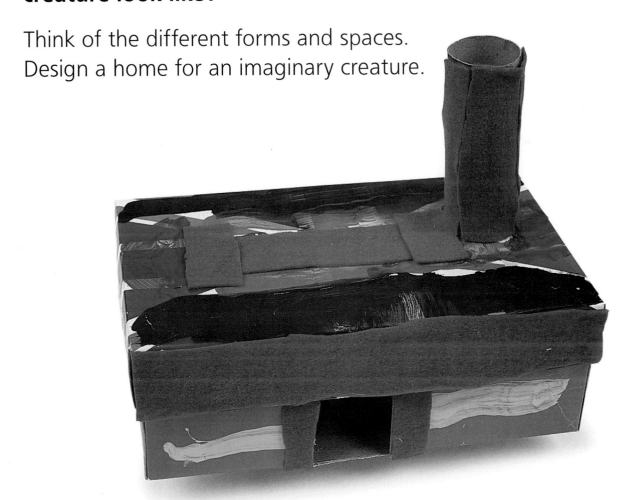

Nick Byers. Age 5. *Rent*. Cardboard and tempera.

The Shapes of Things

Patricia Walker. (American). *Still Life*. Oil on canvas.
22 × 22 inches. Courtesy of Patricia Walker.

Run your finger along the outline of a few objects in this painting. Which objects have similar shapes?

Seeing like an artist

Close your eyes. Would you know a pencil from just touching its shape?

An object has **shape** because of the line around it. The **outline** shows the edges of a shape.

Create

What would the outlines of your favorite shapes look like?

Think of things you'd like to draw. Create a still life using many shapes.

Ali M. Forbes. Age 7. *Apple on a Plate.* Marker and watercolor.

Dance Forms

THE WOOLLOOMOOLOO CUDDLE

1991 © Remy Charlip

Remy Charlip gives drawings of dance positions to people. The people follow the pictures in any order. So everyone does the dance differently!

Dance score of drawings for the dance "Woolloomooloo Cuddle," An Air Mail Dance by Remy Charlip, ©1991.

What To Do

Create a dance from pictures.

1. Look at all the dance moves.

2. Make up a dance from the pictures. Count 1-2-3-4 as you hold each position.

Extra Credit

Find music to go with your dance.
Dance to the music.

Space and Form

Reviewing Main Ides

A form has height, width, and depth.

A form takes up space and has space all around it.

Artist Unknown. (Russian). *Lacquer Box.* 1991. Wood with oil paint and lacquer. Hudak private collection.

Summing Up

An artist made this beautiful wooden box.

Why is the box a form?

Careers in Art

Francie Berger liked to build things with Legos when she was a little girl. Now she is a model designer. She thinks up new things children can build with Legos.

Francie Berger, model designer

Unit 5

An Introduction to
Texture and Rhythm

Winslow Homer. (American). *The Life Line.* (Detail). 1884. Oil on canvas. Philadelphia Museum of Art: George W. Elkins Collection. Philadelphia, Pennsylvania.

Texture is how something feels.
Rhythm is another word for pattern.

This artist shows the textures of things
he paints. He shows rhythm in the pattern
of the waves.

How would the rope and the people's
clothing feel if you could touch them?

Artist Profile

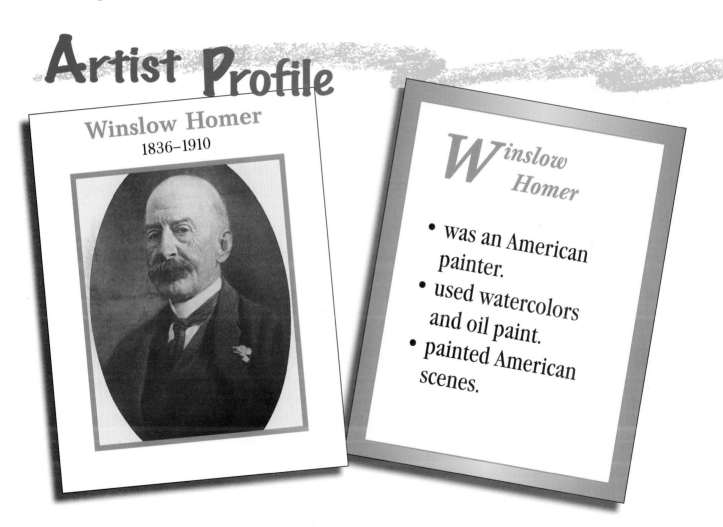

Winslow Homer
1836–1910

*W*inslow
Homer

- was an American painter.
- used watercolors and oil paint.
- painted American scenes.

Real Texture

Some artists use real things in collages. What real things did this artist use?

Kurt Schwitters. (German). *Revolving (Das Kriesen).* 1919. Relief construction of wood, metal, cord, cardboard, wool, wire, leather, and oil on canvas. 48⅜ × 35 inches. The Museum of Modern Art, New York, New York. Advisory Committee Fund. Photograph ©1998 The Museum of Modern Art, New York/©1998 Artists Rights Society (ARS), New York/VG Bild-Kunst, Bonn.

Seeing like an artist

Look around the room. Describe the texture of two objects.

Texture you can feel is called **real texture**. A **collage** has real texture from bits and pieces of things glued onto paper.

Create

What real textures would you put in a collage?

Think of the different textures of the materials you choose. Design a collage.

Joseph Caine. Age 6. *Forms.* Felt paper, string, and material.

Visual Texture

Harold Town. (Canadian). *The First Aeroplane.* 1956. Autographic print on woven paper. 63.7 × 48.4 cm. National Gallery of Canada, Ottawa, Ontario, Canada.

This painting is about a plane. What do you think it would feel like if you touched it?

Seeing like an artist

Describe the textures of things in a picture you like.

Texture you can see but cannot feel is called **visual texture**.

Create

How would you draw something to show how it feels?

Think of how you can capture textures by rubbing. Draw a simple picture to show texture.

Kathryn Lindsey. Age 6. *Textured Drawing.* Crayon and marker.

Carving Real Texture

Artist unknown. (Panama). *Plaque.* 700–1100 A.D. Gold.
22.9 × 21.6 cm. The Brooklyn Museum, New York, New York.
Peabody Museum Expedition to Cocle Province, Panama.

Carved artwork has texture you can feel. Where are the carved lines in this sculpture? What creature do you see?

Seeing like an artist
Look for carved parts in your school walls, floors, and doors.

Artists add real texture to artwork by **carving** and pressing.

Create

How can you show real texture using clay?

Think of a design.
Carve and press real texture.

Blake Herring. Age 7. *Textures*. Clay.

The Texture of People

Johannes Vermeer. (Dutch). *Girl with the Red Hat.* 1665–66. Oil on panel. $9 \times 7\frac{1}{16}$ inches. National Gallery of Art, Washington, DC. Andrew W. Mellon Collection. ©1996 Board of Trustees, National Gallery of Art, Washington, DC.

The artist made the girl in this painting look real. Describe the different textures of her hair, skin, and clothes.

Seeing like an artist

Describe the textures of your hair, skin, and clothing.

Artists sometimes use **visual textures** to paint **portraits**.

Create

How can you make a drawing of yourself using visual texture?

Think of ways to show your different textures. Draw a self-portrait.

Brittany Warren. Age 6. *The Textures of Me in the Leaves.* Crayon and Watercolor.

The Rhythm of Patterns

Artist unknown. Ashanti people (Ghana). *Kente cloth*. From the Girard Foundation Collection in the Museum of International Folk Art, a unit of the Museum of New Mexico, Santa Fe, New Mexico. Photographer: Michel Monteaux.

This artwork has rhythm. Find the repeated shapes, lines, and colors in the cloth.

Seeing like an artist

Where do you see a repeating color in your room?

Repeated shapes, lines, or colors create **visual rhythm** in artwork.

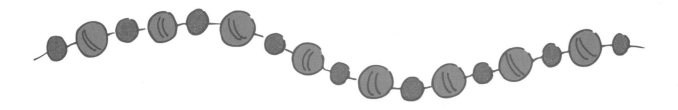

Create

How can you show visual rhythm in a **weaving**?

Think of a fun pattern. Weave it on a paper loom.

Melissa Daigle. Age 6.
Hearts and Spirals. Construction paper and marker.

Changing Rhythm of Patterns

Harry Fonseca. (American). *Coyote Koshare.* 1993. Mixed media on canvas. 24 × 30 inches. Courtesy of Harry Fonseca.

This artwork has many patterns. What patterns are repeated?

Seeing like an artist
Find a pattern on a bookshelf in your classroom.

Every **pattern** has its own **rhythm**.

Create

What kinds of patterns would you design in an artwork?

Think of three designs you like.
Create a pattern.

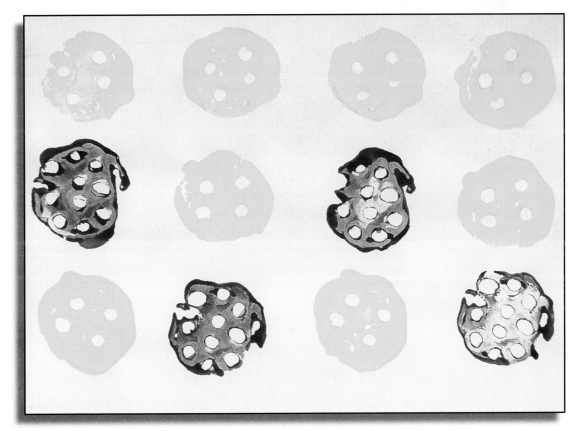

Brian Schmidt. Age 7. *Pattern*. Stamp and tempera.

Texture and Rhythm in Music

John Ramirez is a storyboard artist. He draws pictures to tell stories. John's pictures are often drawn to go with music.

What To Do

Draw pictures to go with music.

1. Close your eyes. Listen to music. Imagine how sea creatures and plants would feel and move to the music.

2. Draw an underwater scene that tells a story about the music you heard.

3. Draw more pictures. Show how the creatures and objects have moved.

Extra Credit

Work alone or with a partner. Make six pictures to show the action in the music.

Texture and Rhythm

Reviewing Main Ideas

You can feel real texture with your hand. You can see visual texture with your eyes.

Repeated colors, lines, or shapes create visual rhythm.

Ellen Day Hale. (American). *June.* c. 1905. Oil on canvas, 24 × 18⅛ inches. The National Museum of Women in the Arts, Washington, DC. Gift of Wallace and Wilhelmina Holladay.

Let's Visit a Museum

This museum is in Washington, DC. It has more than 2,000 artworks by women artists. The museum also has many special activities for children and the community.

Summing Up

This painting has visual texture and rhythm.

What are the textures?

Describe a rhythm in the dress.

National Museum of Women in the Arts, Washington, DC. Photo by Dan Cunningham.

An Introduction to

Emphasis, Balance, and Unity

Leonardo da Vinci. (Italian). *Mona Lisa.* 1503. Oil on wood.
77 × 53 cm. Louvre, Paris, France. Erich Lessing, Art Resource, NY.

Artwork has unity when everything looks like it belongs together. Emphasis is how artists show the most important part in their artwork.

This is one of the most famous paintings in the world. What did the artist emphasize? What colors create unity?

Artist Profile

Leonardo da Vinci
1452–1519

Self Portrait.

Leonardo da Vinci

- was an Italian artist.
- invented the parachute.
- drew plans for a helicopter.

Emphasis on Shape

Miriam Schapiro. (Canadian). *Stepanova and Me, After Gulliver.* 1993. Acrylic and cut paper on canvas. 76 × 43 inches. Steinbaum Krauss Gallery, New York, New York. Private Collection. Photo by Noel Rowe.

Which object is the most important thing in this painting? How does the artist show you?

Seeing like an artist

What shapes are most important on your clothes?

Artists **emphasize** what they feel is most important in their artwork.

Create

How can you show what is important in an artwork of your own?

Think of a shape to emphasize. Design a **collage**.

Libby Cabot. Age 6. *Shape.* Felt paper and marker.

Emphasize the Difference

Artist unknown. (China). *Chinese Children's Slippers*. 1991. Cotton appliqued with silk. $4 \times 2 \times 1\frac{1}{2}$ inches. Hudak Private Collection. Photograph by © Tom Amedis.

The whiskers of these dragon slippers are different from other parts of the dragon. Why do you think the artist made them different?

Seeing like an artist

Describe the difference between the top and the bottom of your shoe.

Artists use **difference** to create **emphasis** in artwork.

Create

What different objects would you use to emphasize a shape in a design?

Think of things you can stitch.
Sew with emphasis.

Elaine Manofsky. Age 7. *Zoey.* Burlap and yarn.

Balance

Artist unknown. Kuna (Panama). *Mola.* Layered and cut
fabric with stitchery. Hudak Private Collection. Photograph by
© Frank Fortune.

Why does this **mola** look balanced?
The animal and lines on the left half match
the animal and lines on the right half.

Seeing like an artist

Look around
you. Is anyone
wearing an evenly
balanced design?

A shape has even **balance** when both halves are exactly the same.

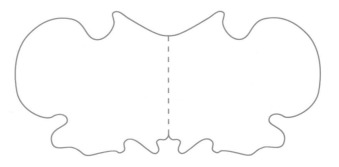

Create

How would you design an artwork to give it balance?

Think of animals and plants you like.
Create an animal and plant design with even balance.

Natalie Flanders. Age 6. *Purple Tulips.* Oil pastel.

Unity in Sculpture

Gilda Snowden. (American). *Monument*. 1988. Encaustic on wood.
193 × 205.7 × 20.3 cm. Detroit Institute of Arts, Detroit, Michigan.
Photograph © 1996 Detroit Institute of Arts, Detroit Artists
Founders Society Purchase, Chaim, Fanny, Louis, Benjamin, Anne
and Florence Kaufman Memorial Trust.

Why do you think the
sculptor repeated the colors
and forms in this artwork?

Seeing like an artist

Are door shapes
repeated through-
out your school?
Are other shapes
repeated?

Colors and forms
that are alike can create
unity in **sculpture**.

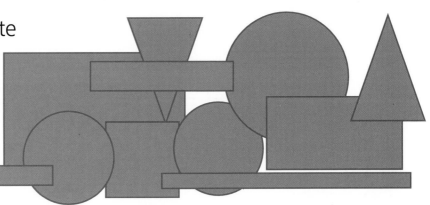

Create

What can you do to show unity in a sculpture?

Think of similar shapes and colors to use.
Design a sculpture that has unity.

Chris Curry. Age 5. *Scott.* Cardboard, marker, and tempera.

Words and Unity

Stuart Davis. (American). *Visa*. 1951. Oil on canvas. 40 × 52 inches. Museum of Modern Art, New York, New York. Gift of Mrs. Gertrud A. Mellon.

This artist uses a few colors, shapes, and words to make a design. What does this painting remind you of?

Seeing like an artist

Name some other places where you see words in artwork.

Colors, shapes, and lines can connect words and pictures to create **unity**.

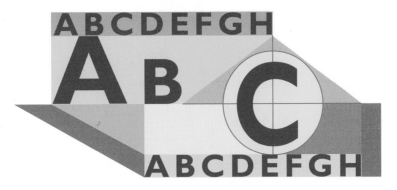

Create

How would you design your own cereal box?

Think of letters, shapes, and colors.
Design a cereal box for your favorite cereal.

Dusty Belk. Age 8. *Coke Man Cereal*. Pencil and oil pastel.

Subjects and Unity

Victor Brauner. (Rumanian). *Prelude to a Civilization.* 1954. Encaustic, and pen and ink, on Masonite. 51 × 79¾ inches. Metropolitan Museum of Art, New York, New York. The Jacques and Natasha Gelman Collection. Photograph by Malcolm Varon. © 1998 Artists Rights Society (ARS), New York/ADAGP, Paris.

Artwork is about things that are important to the artist. What is this artwork about?

Seeing like an artist

What things could you use in a picture about your favorite sport?

A subject can create **unity** in artwork.
The subject connects all the **images**.

Create

How would a mural of your class show unity?

Think of all your classmates together.
Design a **mural** with unity.

Corrinne Loranger. Age 6. *Me.* Crayon.

Unity in Plays

We Tell Stories: Carl Weintraub, waving a scarf as the wind character, in-between two actors in skyscraper costumes.

Carl Weintraub puts on shows for children. He and his actors perform stories from all over the world. The actors help put the stories together.

What To Do

Build a story.

1. Sit in a circle.
   Hold the story stick.

2. Start the story. Give the
   stick to the next person.

3. Go around the circle.
   The last person has
   to end the story.

Extra Credit

Create a story of your own.
Write it down or tell it to a partner.

Emphasis, Balance, and Unity
Reviewing Main Ideas

Colors, shapes, or subjects that are similar can create unity.

Artists use emphasis to show us the most important part of a piece of art.

Lucy Leuppe McKelvey. (American). *Whirling Rainbow Goddesses.* Clay.
12-inch diameter, 6¾ inches high. Keams Canyon Arts and Crafts, New Mexico.

Careers in Art

Lucy Leuppe McKelvey is a potter. She lives in New Mexico. She makes artwork from clay. People buy the beautiful things she makes.

Summing Up

An artist made this pot.

What did she emphasize?

How did she create unity?

Lucy Leuppe McKelvey, potter

Technique Tips

Drawing

Pencil

Make dark lines.   Make light lines.

Crayon

Make thin lines or thick lines.

Make small dots or large dots.

Color in large spaces.

Marker

Make thin lines and small dots with the tip.

Make thick lines with the side of the tip.

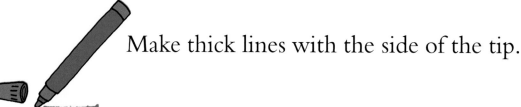

Always replace the cap.

Technique Tips

Oil Pastels

Make lines.

Color in large spaces.

Blend colors.

Colored Chalk

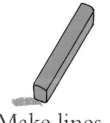

Make lines.

Color in large spaces.

Blend colors.

Technique Tips

Painting

Taking Care of Your Paintbrush

Always rinse before using another color.
Blot it on a paper towel.

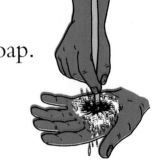

Clean the brush after you paint.

1. Rinse.

2. Wash with soap.

3. Rinse again and blot.

4. Shape the bristles.

5. Store with bristles up.

Technique Tips

Tempera

No drips.

Mix paint on a palette.

Use a wide brush for large areas.

Use a thin, pointed brush for details.

Technique Tips

Watercolor

Put water on each color.

Dip the brush in the paint.

Mix on a separate palette.

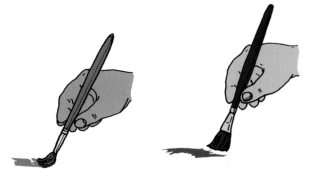

Press firmly for thick lines.

Press lightly for thin lines.

Watercolor Resist

Crayons and oil pastels show through.

Technique Tips

Painting Texture with Watercolor

1. Dip in water.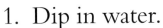

2. Hold brush over container. Squeeze water out.

3. Divide into "spikes."

4. Dip in paint. Lightly touch to paper.

5. Rinse. Shape the bristles in a point.

Technique Tips

Collage

Using Scissors

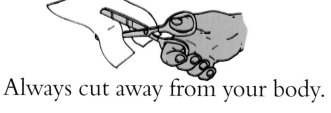

Always cut away from your body.

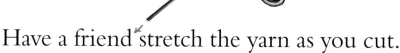

Have a friend stretch the yarn as you cut.

Arranging a Design

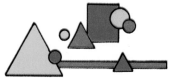

Arrange pieces in a design. Glue them in place.

Using Glue

Use only a few drops to glue papers together.
Smooth with the tip of the glue bottle.
Press the papers together.

Clean the top and close the bottle.

Technique Tips

Printmaking

Making a Sponge Print

Use a sponge for each color.
Dip a sponge in paint.
Press it onto paper.

Making a Stencil

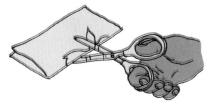

Cut a shape from folded paper.
The empty space is your stencil.

Sponge Printing with Stencils

Hold stencil in place. Press paint into stencil with a sponge.

Technique Tips

Sculpting
Working with Clay

1. Form clay into an oval shape.

2. Squeeze neck.

3. Pull out arms and legs.

Carving Clay

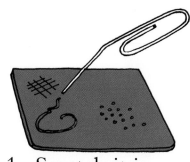

1. Scratch it in.

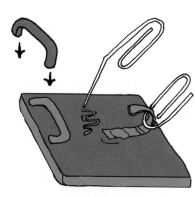

2. Carve it out.

Technique Tips

Paper Sculpture

Making Strip Forms

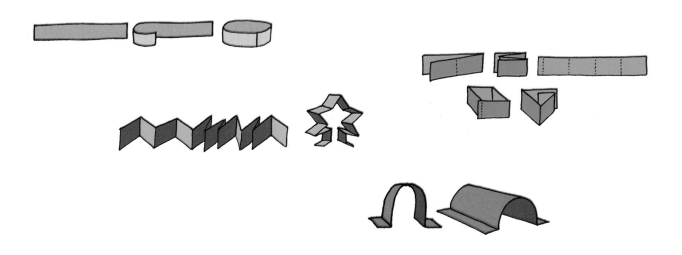

Use to make stairs, stars, fences, and other things.

Cones

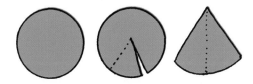

Building with Forms

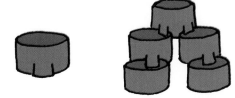

Technique Tips

Needlework

The Running Stitch

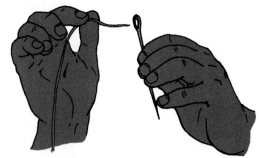

Thread a needle.

Use a running stitch.

Technique Tips

Weaving

Making a Paper Loom

1. Fold paper in half.

2. Cut wide strips from fold.

3. Stop before you reach the top.

Weaving Paper

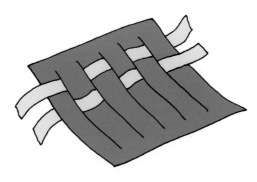

More About...
Art Criticism

Mary Cassatt. (American). *Susan Comforting the Baby.* 1881. Oil on canvas. $25\frac{5}{8} \times 39\frac{3}{8}$ inches. Museum of Fine Arts, Houston, Texas. The John A. and Audrey Jones Beck Collection.

Art Criticism

DESCRIBE

List the people and things you see.

ANALYZE

What lines, shapes, colors, and textures do you see? What part stands out?

More About...
Art Criticism

Mary Cassatt. (American). *Susan Comforting the Baby.* 1881. Oil on canvas. $25\frac{5}{8} \times 39\frac{3}{8}$ inches. Museum of Fine Arts, Houston, Texas. The John A. and Audrey Jones Beck Collection.

Art Criticism

INTERPRET

What is happening? What is the artist telling you about Susan and the baby?

DECIDE

Have you ever seen another artwork like this?

LOOK

Look at the work of art.

Mary Cassatt. (American). *Susan Comforting the Baby.* 1881. Oil on canvas. $25\frac{5}{8} \times 39\frac{3}{8}$ inches.
Museum of Fine Arts, Houston, Texas. The John A. and Audrey Jones Beck Collection.

LOOK AGAIN

Look at the work of art.

What do you think is beyond the edge of the painting?

What sounds do you hear?

LOOK INSIDE

Look at the work of art.

Pretend you are Susan.

Tell a story about this work
of art.

Mary Cassatt. (American). *Susan Comforting the Baby.* 1881. Oil on canvas. $25\frac{5}{8} \times 39\frac{3}{8}$ inches.
Museum of Fine Arts, Houston, Texas. The John A. and Audrey Jones Beck Collection.

LOOK OUTSIDE

Look at the work of art.

How is this like or different from your own life?

What does it make you feel?

What will you remember about this work of art?

More About...
Art History

Artist unknown.
Pagoda of the Temple of the
Six Banyon Trees.
A.D. 537. China.

Artist unknown.
Notre Dame de Paris.
(South Flank).
1400s. France.

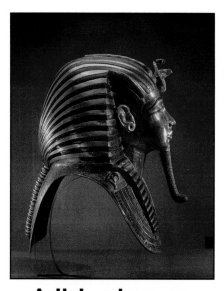

Artist unknown.
Tutankhamen Mask
(side view) Cover.
1340 B.C. Egypt.

Artist unknown.
Parthenon. 448–432 B.C. Greece.

Artist unknown.
Stonehenge.
1800–1400 B.C. England.

Artist unknown.
Yellow Horse. (Chinese Horse). 15,000–10,000 B.C. France.

Artist unknown.
Adena Effigy figure.
1000–300 B.C.
United States.

Artist unknown.
Haniwa Horse.
A.D. 400–500. Japan.

Artist unknown.
Ravenna Apse Mosaic.
(Detail.) A.D. 100. Italy.

Artist unknown.
Shiva, Lord of the Dance.
A.D. 1000. India.

More About...Art History

Leonardo da Vinci.
Mona Lisa. 1503.
Italy.

Claude Monet.
Impression, Sunrise.
1872. France.

Michelangelo.
Head of David.
Italy.

Jan Vermeer.
Girl with the Red Hat. 1660s.
Holland.

Albrecht Dürer.
Self-Portrait.
1500s. Germany.

Artist unknown.
Taj Mahal.
1632–1648. India.

Vincent van Gogh.
Bedroom at Arles.
1888. Holland.

Pablo Picasso.
Gertrude Stein.
1906. Spain.

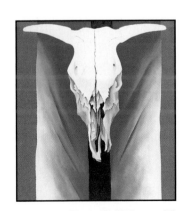

Georgia O'Keeffe.
Cow's Skull, Red, White, and Blue.
1931. United States.

Marc Chagall.
Peasant Life.
Russia.

More About...Art History

More About...
Subject Matter

Artists make art about many subjects. Name the subjects you see on these pages.

Colors and Shapes

Frank Stella. *Silverstone.* ©1996 Collection of the Whitney Museum of American Art, New York, NY. ©1998 Frank Stella/Artists Rights Society (ARS), New York.

More About...
Subject Matter

Things Outside

Claude Monet. *The Parc Monceau, Paris.* Metropolitan Museum of Art, New York.

Everyday Life

Carmen Lomas Garza. *Naranjas (Oranges).* Collection of Mr. and Mrs. Ira Schneider, Scottsdale, Arizona.

More About...
Subject Matter

A Story

People

More About...
Subject Matter

Objects

Jan Brueghel, the Younger.
Still Life: A Basket of Flowers.
Metropolitan Museum of Art,
New York.

Things with a Deeper Meaning

Mary Emmerling.
Heart-shaped "Sailor's Valentine." c. 1830. From *Mary Emmerling's Country Hearts.* ©1988 by Chris Mead, Inc. Reprinted by permission of Clarkson N. Potter, a division of Crown Publishers, Inc.

More About...
Seeing Line Direction

Most pictures you see have lines you
already know.

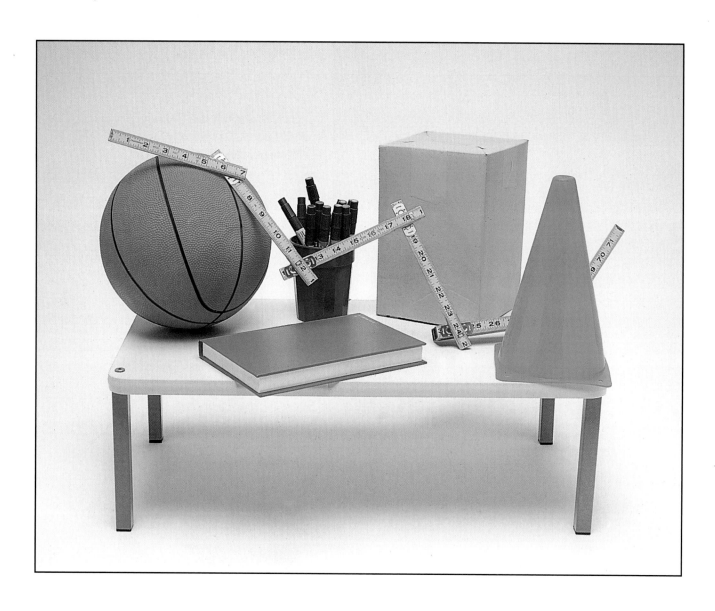

More About...
Seeing Line Direction
LOOK

Look for these lines in the picture.

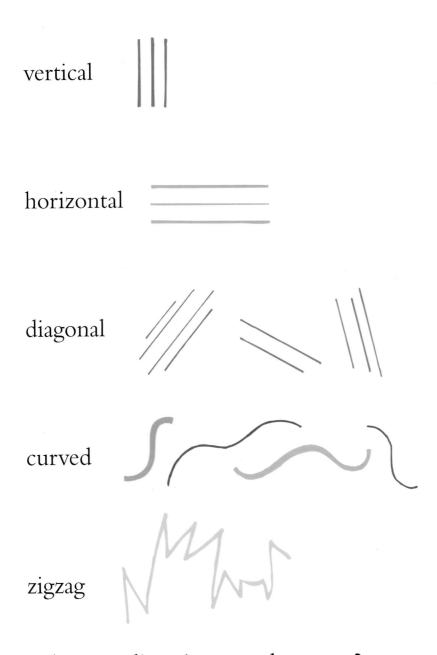

vertical

horizontal

diagonal

curved

zigzag

Where are lines in your classroom?

More About...
Seeing Geometric and Free-Form Shapes

Most pictures you see have shapes you already know.

More About...
Seeing Geometric and Free-Form Shapes
LOOK

Find each geometric shape in the picture.

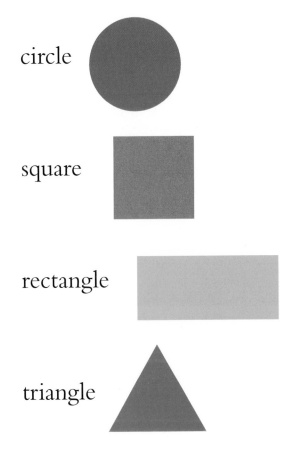

circle

square

rectangle

triangle

Find this free-form shape.

Look for both types of shapes in your classroom.

More About...
Seeing Texture

How would things feel in this picture
if you could touch them?

Seeing Texture

LOOK

What looks rough?

What looks smooth?

What looks fuzzy?

What looks soft?

Find textures in your classroom.

Visual Index: Artworks Arranged in Time Order

Artist unknown
Plaque
A.D. 700–1100
page 90

Jan Vermeer
Girl with the Red Hat
1665–1666
page 92

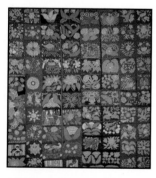

Zeruah Higley Guernsey Caswell
Caswell Rug
1832–1835
page 32

Vincent van Gogh
Bedroom at Arles
1888
page 18

Artist unknown
Corn Palace
c. 1892
page 76

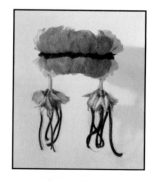

Artist unknown
Man's Headband of Toucan Feathers
c. Twentieth century
page 54

Visual Index

Artist unknown
Kente Cloth
Twentieth century
page 94

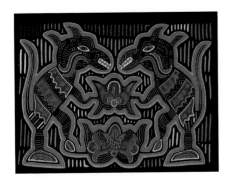

Artist unknown
Mola
Twentieth century
page 108

Lawren S. Harris
Shacks
1919
page 22

Kurt Schwitters
Revolving (Das Kriesen)
1919
page 86

Joaquin Torres-García
New York City—Bird's-Eye View
c. 1920
page 14

Marc Chagall
Peasant Life
1925
page 56

Visual Index

Agnes Tait
Skating in Central Park
1934
page 20

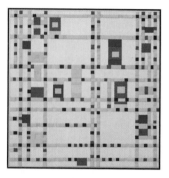

Piet Mondrian
Broadway Boogie-Woogie
1942–1943
page 52

Thomas Hart Benton
July Hay
1943
page 60

Jacob Lawrence
Children at Play
1947
page 24

Henri Matisse
Circus, Plate II from *Jazz*
1947
page 42

Stuart Davis
Visa
1951
page 112

Visual Index

Victor Brauner
Prelude to a Civilization
1954
page 114

Harold Town
The First Aeroplane
1956
page 88

George Sugarman
Yellow Top
1959
page 70

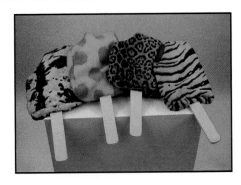

Claes Oldenburg
Soft Fur Good Humors
1963
page 38

Helen Cordero
Storyteller Doll
c. 1964
page 74

Hans Hofmann
Rhapsody
1965
page 58

Visual Index

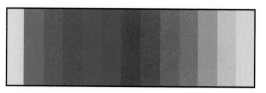

Ellsworth Kelly
Spectrum III
1967
page 50

Nathaniel Bustion
Brownstone Series
c. 1970s
page 72

Roy Lichtenstein
Cubist Still Life
1974
page 40

Jacob Lawrence
Builders—Red and Green Ball
1979
page 36

Frank Stella
Loomings 3X
1986
page 68

Wolf Kahn
Study for *Chesapeake and Ohio Canal in Spring II*
1986
page 16

Visual Index

Carmen Lomas Garza
Naranjas (Oranges)
1988
page 34

Gilda Snowden
Monument
1988
page 110

Artist unknown
Chinese Children's Slippers
1991
page 106

Harry Fonseca
Coyote Koshare
1993
page 96

Miriam Schapiro
Stepanova and Me, After Gulliver
1993
page 104

Patricia Walker
Still Life
1995
page 78

Glossary

architect

Artist who draws and plans buildings.

balance

When both sides look the same.

broken

color wheel

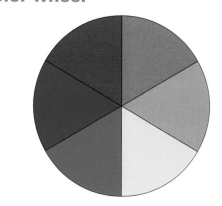

curved (lines)

building

Structures where we live, work, meet, and play.

carving

collage

Bits and pieces of things glued onto paper.

depth

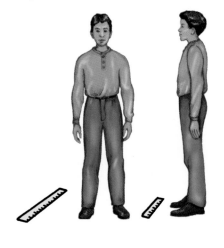

diagonal

Glossary

difference

Something that is not the same.

emphasis

When something stands out, and looks more important.

emphasize

To make something look important.

form

free-form

free-form shape

geometric form

geometric shape

height

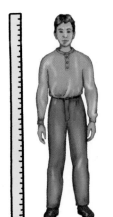

Glossary

horizontal

images

The things you see in an artwork.

line

mola

An artwork in reverse appliqué when layers are cut away after stitching and is sometimes added to clothing.

mural

A painting done on a wall.

outline

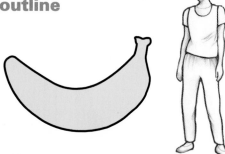

pattern

Repeated shapes, lines, or colors.

portrait

Picture of a person.

position

primary color

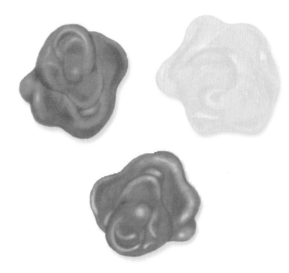

rainbow

Red, orange, yellow, green, blue and purple curved into a semi-circle.

Glossary

real texture

Texture you can feel.

rhythm

rough

sculptor

An artist who makes sculpture.

sculpture

Art that is three-dimensional.

secondary color

shape

smooth

solid (line)

Glossary

space

thin

still life

3-D form

subject

What the artwork is about.

unity

A feeling of belonging together.

thick

vertical

Glossary

visual rhythm

width

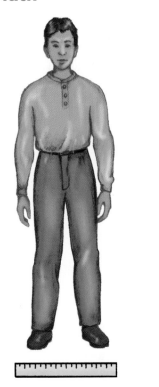

visual texture

Texture you can see but cannot feel.

weaving

Creating fabric by criss-crossing.

zigzag

Index

Index

Index